IMPRINT CLASSICS

Food for Friends

BABETTE HAYES

—

ILLUSTRATED BY FRANCIS YIN

ETT IMPRINT

SYDNEY-PARIS LINK

ETT IMPRINT
PO Box R1906
Royal Exchange NSW 1225
Australia

First published by Rigby in association with Mead & Beckett 1979
New illustrated edition published by ETT Imprint 2017

Reprinted 2018. Colour edition 2021, reprinted 2022
First electronic edition published by ETT Imprint 2017

ISBN 978-1-923024-83-0 (pback)
ISBN 978-1-925706-28-4 (ebook)

A Sydney-Paris Link publication
In memory of Jean-Paul Delamotte

Design by Hanna Gotlieb
Cover shows Babette's "first real kitchen", London 1959

FOR ELIZABETH

— my dear mama

AND FOR ARABELLA

CONTENTS

PREFACE 7

TheStart of it All 19

Rosehip and Apple Jelly 21

EARLY DAYS IN SYRIA 23

Mayonnaise 27

Cheese Souffle 29

Floating Island 31

THE FRENCH EXPERIENCE 34

Rillettes de Tours 36

MY KITCHEN 43

ON SHOPPING 47

THE WAY I SAY I CARE 50

Lassi (Yoghurt Drink) 52

Fresh Peaches with Pureed Fruit 53

Pop Overs 54

Stuffed Pork Fillet Rolls 56

Puree of Zucchinis 58

Potato Casserole 60

Summer Pudding 62

CHRISTMAS 66

Egg Nog 69

Shellfish in Cream Wine Sauce 71

Lamb with Plums 75

Loin of Veal with Cheese 77

Sauteed Potatoes 79

Grapefruit Fluff 81

PICNICS 84

Albert Street Terrine 86

Dada's Orange Picnic Dessert Cake 89

Mulled Wine 91

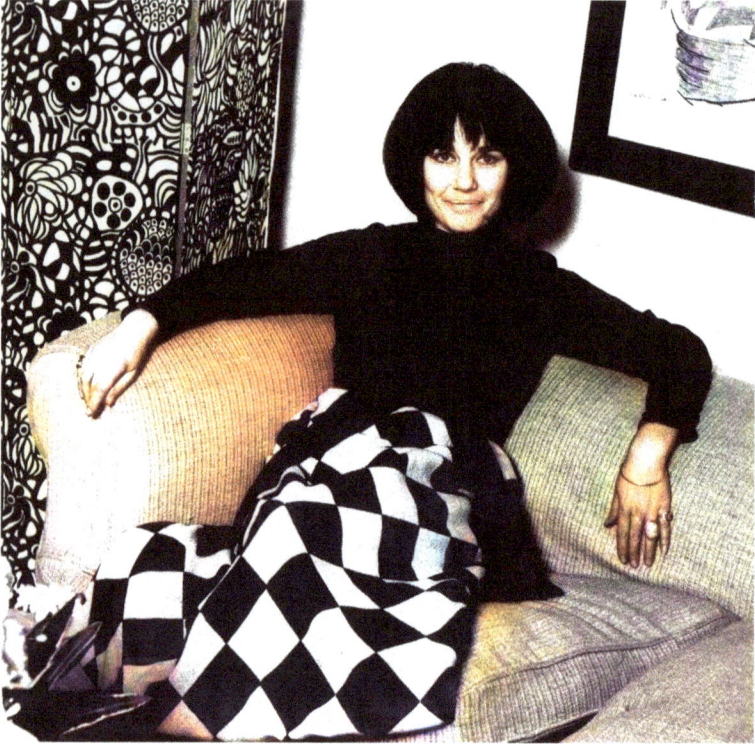

Rodney Weidland's portrait for my book Australian Style, *1969*

Preface

This little book has deep roots in my life in Australia. Along with others by Leo Schofield, Richard Beckett (alias Sam Orr) and Barbara and Charles Blackman, it was first published in 1979, as part of a series of people *'talking about food'*. The series designer, Barbara Beckett, was then married to Richard. She was the driving force behind the books and I suppose, looking back, they were part of an ever-expanding interest in food and what it meant - that was taking place across Australia and in my home town of Sydney. Its publication came at the end of a long decade of research and writing, where I had compiled numerous books and articles on cooking and lifestyle and become much more intimately acquainted with my newly adopted home.

The first venture started shortly after my arrival in Australia in 1965, when I was commissioned by Paul Hamlyn to be the art director and stylist for a hefty tome, the *Australian and New Zealand Complete Book of Cookery*. This involved travelling across both countries and provided a wonderful opportunity for someone who had barely set foot on Australian soil to meet and see what was happening in the world of food and wine 'down under' and 'across the ditch'. At the same time, I had been appointed Cookery Editor for *House and Garden* and Photographic Editor for *Australian Home Journal*.

The next milestone was *200 Years of Australian Cooking*, originally launched as *The Captain Cook Book* to time it with Cook's bicentennial anniversary. It allowed me to extensively research old family diaries and their cooking records. This entailed connecting with members of the Country Women's Association in Tasmania which led to interstate introductions to a wide variety of country women, who loved cooking, and who let me read through their old, treasured, much-used family notebooks and cook books. It also allowed me to meet with famous TV food personalities, who all loved talking about food, and who added a contemporary element.

New publications kept pace with my working life, with *The Home Journal Cook Book* following my appointment as that magazine's Cookery Editor. *The Australian Cook Book in Colour, Barbecue Cooking, Family Fare,* and *Party Fare* all followed. And there was even a Pan paperback, *Babette Hayes Cook Book.* The publication, in 1978, of *Australian Country Cooking Style,* at the encouragement of Barbara Beckett, allowed me to realize another dream – to photograph the food for one of my own cook books. Travelling with various photographers, I had taken photographs with my 35mm Minolta, as I was getting stories together for *Belle* magazine and *Vogue Living,* both interstate and overseas. I enjoyed the responsibility for planning the recipes for *Australian Country Cooking Style,* as well as setting up and gauging the composition and lighting for the finished dishes.

Revisiting the stories and recipes in *Babette Hayes Talks about Food* for this new edition, now titled *Food for Friends,* and featuring my own family photographs, I was asked what has changed in my approach to food. And I realize that I am just as passionate about cooking and eating with family and friends, about sampling food cooked by others, and reading about what is happening in the world of food. I can also sense my early desire to escape from formality in the creek-side picnics in the bush and the informal gatherings described in its pages.

When we first arrived in Australia, I couldn't wait to organise a picnic but was met with resistance. The heat and the flies, I was told, were good reasons for not going ahead. But slowly I convinced our new-found friends

*Off touring through Wales on a camping
holiday in our 1929 Morris Cowley*

that it could be enjoyable, with the right location. I always suggested that they bring a dish they loved making and people would bring their specialities. It was a joy; it was sharing. These events were a reprise of the amazing picnics we'd had in Oxfordshire, setting off in our 1927 Bentley or whatever vintage car we had … packed with food and children, before picking up our friends, Lewis and Patricia Morley, with their young son, Lewis, to meet up with ten or more others at the designated picnic location.

Looking back I see that for me, there has always been a very fine line between friends and family. So these pages recall moments of being together, sometimes gathered around a campfire or, lit by candles, at the kitchen table, in the age-old ritual of enjoying food with loved ones. Reflecting on these many years of cooking and entertaining, I realize that I like not to be too formal. I like to mix things on the table … plates and wine glasses that don't really match. If people want to help, I like to have them around me, catching up on news as they chop and stir or whatever. We rarely had a separate dining room and it still doesn't appeal because I am not going to shut myself away somewhere just because I am cooking. And there is a certain pleasure in having a sense of support and help. For their part, friends and family also enjoy sharing, and maybe learning, although that has never been the intention. I think you can cook anything anywhere, even on a camp fire. I would liken it to someone who is comfortable with words, spoken or written, which flow with ease them. Cooking is a part of me. It flows for me and I feel totally comfortable with it.

Those who know me, know of my childhood. I was born in Damascus and we lived in Douma in a typical, large, flat-roofed home, surrounded by a lush green garden. Brief holiday visits to the Lebanon were frequent and when my father died in battle, in Syria, in 1941, we lived in Cairo and Alexandria. This period of my life ended when I was finally taken to England, aged 8, by my mother and my new stepfather, on a troopship in December 1944, towards the end of the war.

I arrived in England, not speaking a word of English. All school children were evacuated due to the bombing of London and the major cities, so after a brief spell in the North of England, I was sent to a boarding school to learn the correct King's English. I was strictly brought up from

(Top) Family picnic amongst the ruins with my friends in Syria 1939; (lower) In Hyde Park, London, with my brother Bruno, wearing our boarding school uniforms 1946

'day one' and quickly had to learn perfect English table manners. I was not to speak at the table during mealtime and I curtsied every time I was introduced to an adult until I was 14 years old.

Post-war, when my mother was working at the French Consulate and was usually very tired, I would help her prepare the meal, clear away and wash up. She was an invalid for a while in England, following a back operation, and was unable to move around very much. So, from the age of eleven, I did the weekly family shopping regardless of whether we lived locally or across the Thames, in Barnes.

I learnt to negotiate with our grocer In Kings Road Chelsea to swap food coupons in our ration books - saving our soap stamps to buy precious eggs and negotiating with the grocer to procure other rare rations like butter. Mama was regularly getting *Elle,* one of the top French magazines, and I loved their food articles, collecting the recipes and recipe cards they published every week. Each card would give you their suggested three course daily menus, which I pored over and practised where possible. I had never previously researched cooking methodology other than learning to cook my mother's specialities which all involved eggs – dishes that she would get our cook in Syria to prepare for the many menus she would organise for VIPs and their visitors: Cheese *souffle,* vanilla egg custard for *Ile Flottante,* fish and prawns with cream sauce, *Quiche Lorraine, Mousse au Chocolat.* The rest I learned by experience, by making use of whatever I had or whatever was available - by whatever came up; whatever presented itself.

When I was 15, I went to Hammersmith Art School in London, where it seemed natural for me to go to our local Shepherd's Bush food market to get lunch for fellow students, then come back to put out a feast, at minimal cost, for 8-10 of us. I would also cook for my friends at home. My Austrian stepfather owned a factory making underwater swimming gear and I would organise working bees, where we put together underwater masks to earn much-needed pocket money. We would sit in my bedroom, working away, before I went down to cook a budget spaghetti or rice dish. It was always such a joy to sit and eat together.

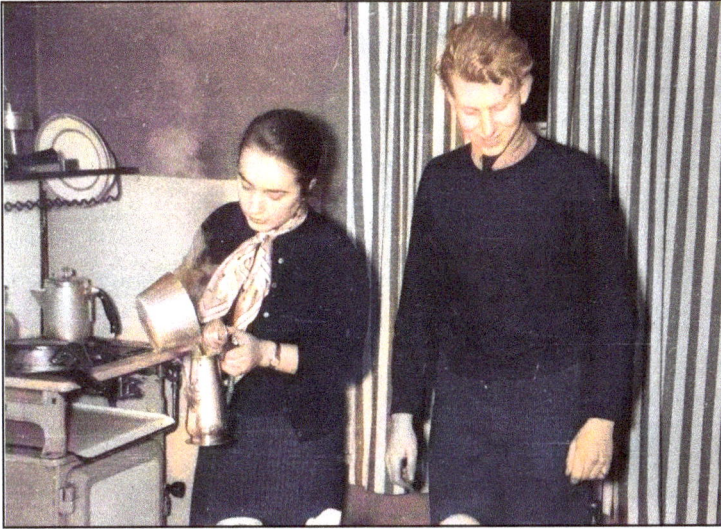

*(Top) Our first kitchen about to serve coffee 1957; (Lower)
Farewells with my mother as Stephanie, Guy and I are about to
sail from Portsmouth on the SS Canberra, January 1965*

Over these years, I adapted myself to whatever kitchen was at hand and I have had a series of kitchens in my life, none of them the 'ideal, dream, functional, beautiful kitchen' and definitely not the kitchens I have carefully designed for my various clients, after this became my design speciality. But every kitchen of my own has been much appreciated, even when it was not like our latest, super-efficient kitchen in the house at the back of *The Hospital Shop*, where we are living in Bowral. But I would say that, whatever the kitchen you are faced with, you can learn to work with it.

Talk of kitchens makes me recall my first one as a young married woman in Shepherd's Bush on three half-levels of a workman's tiny terrace house. We had two bedrooms, one minute bathroom, one living room and a very basic kitchen. It had a small fridge and stove lined up along one wall, alongside a sink with no hot water; we carried it in from the bathroom next door. On the opposite wall to the sink, there was a small Victorian-era fireplace, with shelves either side. In between, there was just enough room for a small jewel of a round, antique, scrubbed-pine table with four chairs, given to us by Mimi, my husband's mother. We would stretch the seating with stools and somehow managed to squeeze six to eight people around it.

In London, I was working for *Josiah Wedgwood* on their showroom and exhibition displays, enjoying their range of historic and contemporary dinnerware and visiting their 'seconds' factory for bargain buys. As I started styling for various home magazines, I found myself writing on cooking for *Queen Magazine*, and moved on to be the cookery writer for the newly launched *Sunday Telegraph Colour Magazine*, with the 'test' cooking taking place in the most humble of kitchens, ours!

In Sydney, after I emigrated here with my husband, Guy, and two-year-old daughter Stephanie in 1965, my 'test' kitchen became the small 1930s kitchen we had in a flat overlooking Mosman's Sirius Cove. I recall waking up on our first day to the sound of fishermen, casting nets from their bright, Mediterranean blue and green painted boats – a dream come true. That small kitchen was soon put to work as I was appointed cookery editor for *House and Garden*. I did all the dishes for

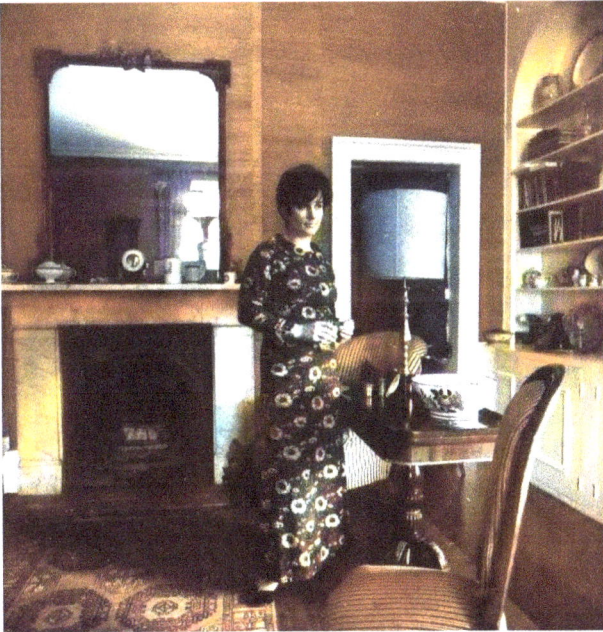

(Top) Our first makeshift kitchen in the laundry at Hunters Hill 1967; (Lower) Hunters Hill 1968

my cookery articles there, which were photographed as I cooked and styled in our home and garden.

Two years later, we bought our first home. It was in Hunters Hill and we moved in with our two young children, Stephanie and baby Sholto – Arabella was yet to come. It was a wonderful old sandstone house with a long, wide verandah at the back that everyone remembers for the memorable meals we shared there at our very long table, often seating 16.

We eventually put in a new kitchen, using pine for the joinery, which was set against old sandstone walls and complimented by a terracotta floor of round, inverted drain-pipe caps – the closest thing I could devise to my French Grandmother's hexagonal tiles. Two ovens were a 'must', along with a wide gas cook-top, over which sat a magnificent copper hood, made by my friend, master-craftsman, Louis Berczi. A round antique Australian cedar table sat in the middle and was used for our family meals as well as doubling up as much-needed work space. With its stable door and graceful old windows - the original ceiling rafters overhead – this kitchen was a warm setting for many a photoshoot for several cook books over the next 16 years.

Then it was time to take a break from the magazine, design, book-writing world. Meditation, and a different pace of life saw me returning to England in 1984 for a few years before I found myself heading back to Mosman and living, once again, in an old stone house. I picked up where I had left off, writing, designing, exploring and enjoying the changing world of food and cooking, and appreciation of what Australia offered in design and architecture.

Twenty-five years later, I have moved on to another adventure with my youngest daughter, Arabella, who had always wanted to run a café and shop. In 2015, following a phone call from an old friend, Jasper Foggo, we came to a new life in Bowral, as owners of *The Hospital Shop* in Mona Road, which is next to Bowral Hospital. This latest adventure has been quite a learning curve and most of all we have enjoyed being part of the community and making many new friends. I have particularly appreciated our super-efficient, light-filled kitchen in the house that lies at the back of the café.

(Top) Interviewing Christo in New York for Belle 1979 (photograph by Lewis Morley); (Lower) My trio: Arabella, Sholto and Stephanie

But location aside, some things remain central to me. I enjoy bringing people together; both old friends and new acquaintances. If I have any wish it is just to pass on the pleasure of sharing and seeing information passed on to others. It gives me great joy to see my daughters, Stephanie and Arabella, cooking, and also my granddaughter, Hanna, trying new recipes. For his part, my son Sholto is particularly good at cooking chops and steak. He has the perfect touch and knows how to seal in the juices and cook so it is as rare as we each individually like it. He also does magical things with the river trout he catches, which he pan fries on a camp fire or smokes in his smoking box, and if we are lucky, brings to cook for us to enjoy at home.

I have enjoyed my personal cooking journey from the changes that took place in England in the 1950s with the influence of inspiring writers like Mapie de Toulouse Lautrec in *Elle*, to Elizabeth David's adventures as she wrote about her food discoveries and travels through France, Italy and Spain – all so transforming to England's attitudes to cooking. Then coming to Australia in 1965 opened so many doors. The timing was perfect, offering me many publishing opportunities to express new ideas. Through magazines and books, I was able to reach a wide readership, offering me the privilege to be able to contribute to Australian culture in so many ways. I felt deeply honoured when, on the Queen's birthday, in June 2014, I was awarded the Order of the Medal of Australia (OAM) for Service to Interior Design, Australian Cuisine and writing (books and articles).

It has been an adventure which has led to personal and professional friendships with various ground-breaking food writers and visionaries, committed 'foodies', organic farmers and cheesemakers, creative photographers, designers, artists, architects and inspiring home makers. Of these, none has been more sustaining that my lasting friendship with my dear friend, Margaret Fulton, who has made such an immense impact on Australians and influenced generations of families.

But finally, my personal journey has been about much more than the cooking. It has been about the preparation and being together, and creating together an embracing experience as an ordinary part of our everyday lives.

The start of it all

With my marriage I acquired a delightful, understanding mother-in-law. Mimi's influence greatly contributed to my personal development. Not only does she have a creative streak, which was evident in the way she set up her many homes around the world, but the structure of her American upbringing has filtered through in many other areas. Certainly it is through her that I developed a taste for English food and extended my vision beyond French cuisine to the wholesome and adventurous cooking of England and the United States. The many years Mimi spent in Spain and Italy also influenced her cooking style and enlarged her culinary repertoire. She encouraged my eclectic collecting instincts whether it was in the accumulation of recipes, ideas, antiques, furniture or furnishings.

When I was newly-wed we spent our first holiday in the Lake District — a particularly beautiful part of England close to the northern border where the rugged framework of the Scottish landscape is overlayed by the softer quality of the English countryside. There are lakes, mountains, stone walls, stone cottages — all the components for evocative appealing scenery.

We rented a small cottage without electricity; kerosene lamps provided the lighting and for cooking there was a marvellous fuel stove. This was my first confrontation with an Aga cooker and I was keen to experiment and take advantage of it. My parents-in-law were coming home on leave from Hong Kong and were to join us for a week. Here was the chance for me to impress Mimi with something special.

A prune souffle would be a fitting climax for our first meal together as a family. The preparations went smoothly, the oven was at the right temperature, into it went the souffle, and I sat back and waited. After the prescribed time I proudly lifted it out of the oven to carry it to the table. But where was the light-as-a-feather souffle proudly peering five centimetres above the rim of the dish? In its place was a curious cake-like object at the bottom of the dish. Undaunted, I thought we should at least sample the failure as I was reluctant to throw it away. But the leather-hard surface resisted all my attempts at cutting and chiselling. Mimi and I giggled uncontrollably. All signs of tension disappeared; the ice was broken.

I stopped worrying about having to impress my in-laws and made up for it by cooking kilograms of rosehip and crab-apple jelly during the remainder of our stay. A fascinating almost unreal quality enhances crab-apples, which are perfect little miniature apples. They are so exquisitely proportioned and delicately coloured they look too good to eat. Masses and masses of jelly were made in the most ideal circumstances, slowly cooked in the steady low heat of the Aga's oven.

ROSEHIP AND APPLE JELLY

The enjoyment of picking rosehips - nature's bounty - is followed by the great pleasure of turning them into a delicious, fragrant and very countrified jelly.

Crab-apples are the best to use. Windfalls will do very well providing any bruised and damaged areas are cut out, and the greener the better is the maxim. The rosehips must be just right and not crinkled.

For 2 kilograms of prepared apples you will need 1 kilogram of rosehips. Don't peel the apples, simply chop them coarsely. Put them into your largest saucepan or preserving pan and cover with water; then add 750 millilitres of water. Bring to the boil and cook until pulpy. Meanwhile coarsely mince the rosehips. Add to the apples and simmer very gently for 10 minutes. Remove them from heat, and leave them to steep for another 10 minutes. Strain the fruit through a sterilised jelly bag. (A muslin cloth or teatowel will do.) Leave overnight undisturbed to drip into a large bowl. Don't squeeze or you will cloud the mixture.

For every 2 ½ cups (8oz cups 20 metric ounces of liquid) add 400 grams of sugar.

This country tip was given to me in the Lake District. Heat the sugar in the oven before adding it to the mixture. Bring the juices to the boil and boil rapidly far 3 to 4 minutes; add the hot sugar and boil until the mixture jells. Test on a cold saucer. Then pour the liquid into sterilised heated jars, cover and label. Store in a cool dark place.

When still a schoolgirl, I had collected every recipe I could find in Elle magazine. And I still have those scrapbooks; they are a reminder of a passionate interest in food which had few opportunities of expression.

The French are very concerned about their food and they search endlessly for variety. There is no such thing as the same roast every Sunday, followed by curried left-overs the next day, mince on Tuesday and so on. I was impressed by Mapie de Toulouse-Lautrec's weekly contributions to Elle of menus, giving three and four course meals for lunch and dinner seven days a week.

The next important influence on my cookbook reading was Elizabeth David. I immediately loved, and have continued to love, her easy writing style, her honesty and thoroughness in her approach to food.

It is curious how much influence women have had in establishing a high standard in the culinary arts. Am I waving the flag? Why not? I am frequently asked why it is that male chefs have dominated the scene. Yet for more than two hundred years, women, through the written word, have had a greater influence than men in teaching millions of people the art of cooking. Names such as Elizabeth Raffald, Eliza Acton, Mrs Beeton, Mapie de Toulouse-Lautrec, Elizabeth David, Margaret Costa, Jane Grigson, Julia Child and Simone Bert- holt, to list just a few, have made a big impression on households around the world, and in Australia Margaret Fulton has had a lasting influence and will continue to do so.

I was born in Syria, where we led a comfortable life, and later moved to Egypt and England. As a child I helped my mother during her bouts of illness and when she worked extremely long hours. Suddenly she found herself widowed, in dire circumstances, and solely responsible for the keep and welfare of two children. Then my mother remarried, I lived in London with her and my English stepfather, and my brother lived with relatives in France.

I learnt to shop wisely and to balance and juggle the ration coupons. At times we led a somewhat nomadic existence moving from flat to bedsitter. But we were always faithful to our grocer in Chelsea, where I was able to exchange soap coupons for eggs and other hard-to-get goodies. By the age of eleven I had gutted my first chicken, cooked my first Christmas dinner and generally learnt to make myself very useful.

Early days in Syria

My mother's cooking experience, until she found herself in England, consisted of planning elaborate menus for dinner parties during her happy years in Syria. She had also taught herself, and subsequently taught me, to make several superb dishes.

She talks of our life in Syria in the 'thirties and 'forties with all the outrage and horror of a sophisticated Frenchwoman in a foreign land and still manages to make it sound terribly romantic. Delve further and one finds that it was not so easy for Europeans to fit into a village setting on the edge of a desert.

We lived in the tiny village of Douma, some twenty-five kilometres from Damascus. We had a large house there with high, high ceilings, no gas or electricity and our garden water supply was drawn from a huge well in the large kitchen. Drinking water was fetched daily from the public pump at Damascus.

My father, a Frenchman, had made the army his career. He was originally sent to Syria for three years. As Political Officer he had under his jurisdiction a large area around Damascus.

He and my mother were frequently entertained by sheiks and the meals that took place were ritualistic and unchanging. Guests would arrive at eleven or so for lunch; the sheep was killed and cooked as soon as you

*Our family in our Damascus garden, my brother
Bruno on Maman's knee, 1939*

arrived. As the process took some time, lunch would not begin for about three hours. Meanwhile, the mezze (hors d'oeuvres) would be served: black olives, green olives, sliced tomatoes and cucumbers, and the 'most revolting peas, discoloured, swimming in that frightful mutton fat'. The cooked sheep was eventually brought in. The guests of honour were always offered the sheep's eyes as a mark of the highest esteem. My mother, who soon lost her liking for mutton and lamb — 'you can imagine how tough the sheep were,' she said — had cleverly established a reputation for being a very small eater, and always managed somehow to decline without offending.

'You just prayed to God you could swallow it down,' she said. 'It would have been unthinkable to refuse.'

Damascus is surrounded with apricot and almond orchards and the Syrians make a paste with the apricots, which was in those days exported to Turkey and Europe. The method of manufacture would seem somewhat primitive and basic to Western hygiene-conscious eyes. The trees would be given a good shake and the fruit left where they fell, maggots and flies being allowed their share of the feast. Then the fruit was gathered, taken to various homes and put into a primitive mill, the handle was laboriously turned and the ensuing pulp came out of a pipe into a bucket. The mixture was poured onto trays and left to dry in the sun. It was then cut into thick cakes of about eight by twenty-four centimetres, packed in Cellophane and sent off.

Raisins were tipped into ditches. 'The donkeys and camels roamed around there too,' recounts my mother in her delicious, very French voice. 'And the raisins were left there to dry.' Then they were shaken, packed and sent to Europe. She has never touched a raisin since.

What did Europeans eat in Syria? My parents were renowned for their hospitality and my mother loved to hold dinners for fourteen, sixteen, or more. (I sometimes think I inherited from her my own love of dinner parties.) These dinners would usually follow a day's shoot, which yielded a bag of gazelles (delicate deerlike creatures) and gata. The gata were similar to English partridge.

We cooked the gata very much as one would a partridge, while the gazelles were skinned and left to 'become tender' in the vast icebox off the kitchen. A spit was built in the garden; it had a large hole underneath for the fire, for the purpose of roasting gazelles. As these animals have a rather dry meat, they would first be larded with pieces of fat and then placed on the spit, where the Arab staff took it in turns to turn the handle.

There was no question of using local vegetables other than tomatoes or cucumbers. The quality was poor and we relied on the best tinned vegetables from France such as tiny peas and young thin French beans. Menus were planned by mother and our cook, Joseph.

Meals were relatively simple, very French in presentation and style. My mother had been brought up in an academic atmosphere and was not very domesticated. However, there were a few things she excelled in and always made a point of preparing herself, such as mayonnaise, cheese souffle and a dessert called Floating Island, made with a custard rich in eggs.

MAYONNAISE

Mayonnaise is the easiest of sauces to make, and it is difficult for me to accept that it is necessary to buy it ready made. Certainly the thick sweet and sour sauce that goes under the guise of that name bears no resemblance to its namesake and is more like a salad cream.

I make up a large quantity and put it in airtight containers in a cool spot. It does not need to be refrigerated unless the weather is very hot and humid. The flavour and texture can be varied by adding a whipped egg white per cup of mayonnaise, or half a cup of whipped cream. Add lots of freshly chopped herbs or minced gherkins and capers. Some finely chopped fresh basil or tarragon is delicious too. Add more lemon juice or a little good wine vinegar flavoured with a herb. The tomato puree turns it into something else again. The permutations are endless. But I prefer the straight mayonnaise and find it particularly delicous over some cold hard-boiled eggs, with cold cuts of meat or served with cold boiled zucchinis that have been marinated in a french dressing.

For a large jar of mayonnaise:
4 large egg yolks
2 heaped tablespoons Dijon mustard, or more to taste
750 ml olive oil
Salt
¼ cup lemon juice, or 1 to 2 tablespoons good wine vinegar

Put the egg yolks and the mustard into a pudding basin and using a whisk, a small electric egg beater or a wooden spoon, stir until amalgamated and then start dripping the oil, drip by drip until it 'takes' and becomes thick. Once the mixture becomes thick, you can add the oil in a steady stream. If you add too much oil too quickly at first, the mixture will curdle.

When the oil has been used up, a little more oil can be added, if needed. Adjust the salt content. (Dijon mustard is pretty salty so I usually add the salt at the end, but tastes vary.) Lastly, beat in the lemon juice or vinegar, and put the mayonnaise into airtight containers if not using it straightaway.

If for some reason the mixture does curdle, revive it by starting with an egg yolk in a clean bowl and then dripping in the curdled mixture a little at a time until it has thickened.

In our glorious garden in Douma, with Bruno, playing my banjo 1939

CHEESE SOUFFLE

My mother preferred to serve this in one large splendid souffle dish. There would be 'oohs' and 'aahs' as the dish was carried into the dining-room, and it never failed to make an impression. The quantity given below serves six. If you have twelve people to serve, make two souffles and don't forget to serve it as soon as it is ready. The centre should be just a little creamy, and the outside firm but certainly not dry.

40 g butter

50 g flour

1 ¼ cups milk

30 g Parmesan cheese, grated

120 g Gruyere or Emmenthaler cheese, grated

Salt and freshly ground pepper

¼ teaspoon cayenne pepper (optional)

6 eggs, separated

Melt the butter and stir in the flour until smooth. Cook for 2 minutes, stirring. Remove from the heat, add a little of the milk and stir until smooth. Return to heat and continue to add the rest of the milk, stirring all the time. Cook on a low heat for 10 minutes. Add the cheese, season to taste, and mix well. Cool a little.

Beat the egg yolks into the mixture. Beat the egg whites until stiff and firm, and fold into the cooled cheese mixture, using a metal spoon. Do this quickly and lightly, using as few movements as possible.

Pour the mixture into a preheated, buttered souffle dish and bake in the hottest part of the oven at 180°C (350°F) for 25 to 35 minutes. The time depends on the individual oven, also on the width and depth of the souffle dish and the accuracy of the thermostat. My gas oven cooks this mixture to a creamy-centre state in 30 minutes.

FLOATING ISLAND

Floating Island is a dessert that seems to take people back in time. It is old-fashioned, rich, delicious and sweet.

Allow 6 egg yolks and 1 whole egg or 9 to 10 egg yolks per litre of milk (save the egg whites for the Snow)

2 vanilla pods, or 1 ½ tablespoons real vanilla essence 5 heaped table-spoons white sugar

For 6 people you will need 9 large fat Italian sponge fingers or 18 French ones, and 1 quantity of the above mixture

Cream of tartar, Brandy, Extra milk

To make the custard

Heat the milk up slowly with the vanilla pods (split in two) and the sugar. The vanilla pods must be allowed to steep in the milk to get the full flavour. When they are steeped, take out and wash and put away when dry. If using vanilla essence, just heat the milk with the essence and sugar to scalding point.

Have the egg yolks and eggs ready in a large mixing bowl and just lightly beat to amalgamate, but do not beat to a froth. Pour the very hot milk over the eggs, beating all the time to blend it thoroughly. Pour the mixture back into the hot pan and put on the lowest heat possible, stirring non-stop or the mixture will curdle. As a custard mixture will collect on the bottom and sides of a pan, you cannot leave a custard on its own, and you cannot put it on anything other than the lowest heat. As soon as the mixture coats the back of a spoon, the custard is ready. (Draw a line along the back of the spoon and if the line stays, the custard is ready.) To slow down the cooking process, pour the custard out of the pan straightaway and into a large mixing bowl. Taste the custard to make sure the sweetness is to your liking. Add a little more sugar if necessary.

To make the Snow

Have ready a wide shallow saucepan or deep frying-pan of boiling water. I like my Snow unsweetened, but others may like it sweet, if so beat some sugar into egg whites.

Beat the egg whites in a copper bowl until very firm. If you don't use a copper bowl, add a pinch of cream of tartar. When the egg whites are really firm, spoon the mixture on to the simmering boiling water to poach it. Turn it over after 60 seconds, taking care not to break up the mixture too much, and poach another 30 seconds. Take out with a slotted spoon and place on a strainer or colander, and repeat this process until all the egg whites are done, using 1 to 2 strainers or colanders. Keep poached egg whites intact if possible.

To put together

Some good brandy and milk is needed to dip the sponge fingers in. The ratio is ¼ cup brandy to ¾ cup milk. Put into a dish that will comfortably take the length of a sponge finger. Quickly dip each one into the brandy and milk. Put a row of 4 or 5 fingers on the bottom of a serving bowl and spoon a little of the custard over them; then place another layer of dipped fingers on top, stacking them in the opposite direction. Use up all the sponge fingers, putting a little spoonful or two of the custard between each layer. Make an *even tower of sponge fingers, gently pour the custard around the sponge fingers and spoon the Snow over the top, dribbling the remaining custard over the top.*

Damascus in 1939 was blessed with the services of a cremerie run by a white Russian who had escaped the Revolution. The produce came from his farm on the outskirts of Damascus and was the only place where you could find cows milk, butter, cream, bread and beef. The only items my mother ever bought from the market were pistachios and almonds — in their shells of course!

Things have changed since then no doubt, and I would love to go back there in the spring and autumn to investigate the food scene and find out if the smell of hot mutton fat is still rampant and rancid as it was in my childhood.

The French Experience

Countless experiences spring to mind that are directly associated with food. And each and every one of the occasions have been shared with someone or several people. So I tend to associate people with food, food with people. As I was born in Syria and then moved to Egypt and on to England, at the age of twelve I still had not known the joys of France or met my uncles, aunts and cousins of the Bayle clan. Yet my upbringing was French and our meals were French.

My first visit to France was a joyous occasion, a reunion with my brother and an introduction to my large family. The food experience was a revelation to the eye and the palate. Even though the post-war, highly improvised bread inevitably contained some far from pleasant foreign matter and was referred to as 'black', it tasted remarkably good with the sausages and terrines the charcutier had to offer. There were cheeses which I had never known before: delectable petit suisses (small, smooth-as-silk cream cheeses), pastries, ice creams and an incredible variety of fruit and vegetables and, of course, fresh butter and cream.

We picked wild strawberries amid the wild cyclamen in the wood adjoining my grandmother's house. My first sight of a country kitchen totally won me over, as did my darling little grandmother. She produced some wonderful food such as a light creamy cheese custard covered with mushroom sauce made with wild mushrooms.

On Sundays there would be long walks through the vineyards to go to church; it was difficult, and in fact well nigh impossible to resist the temptation to surreptitiously sneak a few grapes, and hope God wasn't looking!

My tiny aunt who was as greedy as I was, managed to obtain all sorts of local goodies: rillettes, a goose, rabbits marinated and cooked with prunes and wine and then the juices reduced (washed down with a local white wine, the famous Vouvray).

RILLETTES DE TOURS

It would, be difficult not to include a recipe from my family hometown, Tours, famous for its rillettes, an exceedingly rich meat paste that is rarely made at home, but bought at the local charcutier, where only foodstuffs made from pork are sold. Every small town and village have their own version. The competition is brisk and comparisons are always being made to decide who makes the best. A visit to France, for me, always means visiting aunts and uncles and having delightful family meals that unswervingly include at least one, if not two, samplings of rillettes.

If you want to make a large quantity, use a suckling pig. The rillettes keep well once potted, rather like preserved goose. In fact a mixture of halfgoose arid half pork is called rillettes d'oie.

500 g pork fat from the loin or fat areas of pork

500 g belly of pork, rind and bones removed

500 g lean fat free pork

1 ½ tablespoons salt mixed with ½ teaspoon mixed spice - cinnamon, allspice and cloves

Preheat oven to 180°C (350°F).

Coarsely mince the pork fat, put in bottom of cast-iron casserole, season and lay the bones from the belly on top. Cut the belly of pork into small dice, scatter evenly on top of fat, and season with the salt and the spice. Cut the lean meat into small child-size fingers, season, and cover with the pork rind; put the lid on and put in the middle of the oven. Turn oven down to 130°C (275°F). Bake for 1 ¾ to 2 hours. Do not stir or disturb. Take the bones and the rind out. Cool a little and start to shred the meat apart with two forks. The meat must be shredded to give that typical string paste look. When perfectly shredded, put into deep pottery bowl or jars. The fat will come to the top, sealing and preserving the meat. When cold, cover with circles of greaseproof paper, tie with string and store in cool larder or refrigerator. Serve with fresh crusty bread — you won't need any butter.

If using a suckling pig, the procedure is the same. Simply separate the fat, the bones and the meat, use a wider-bottomed cast-iron pan. Mince the fat, cut the bones into smallish pieces and cut the meat into finger-size strips. Place in layers, fat, bones, meat — more salt and spice will be necessary. Cooking time will be about 3 ½ to 4 hours. Traditionally the cooking is done on top of the stove, covered, very gently simmered, and the contents are not disturbed. Once cooked, the bones are taken out, the heat raised underneath the pot and the mixture stirred and stirred until all the moisture has evaporated. It is then potted, cooled, covered and stored.

Food in the country was not nearly as scarce as in the cities and there certainly seemed to be a great deal more of everything compared to sad old London.

Two years later, when I was fourteen years old, I returned to France for another twelve weeks of blissful summer holidays. This time I stayed with one of my father's many brothers and his family in a rambling old house and surgery near Orleans, of Joan of Arc fame. It had a huge walled courtyard at the rear with numerous rabbit hutches filled with lovely fluffy white rabbits. 'What marvellous pets,' I thought until I realised they were being bred for the table. I avoided the execution and preparation for the pot, but was more than happy to sample the dish. I had a passion for petit suisse sprinkled with castor sugar and eaten on their own or with wild strawberries — they were sublime. I would sneak into my room with a box of six so I didn't have to share them around!

It was here that the difference between the French and the English approach to food was made obvious to me. Imagine the scene on an average day . . .

At breakfast, the long table in the dining-room is spread with a checked cloth. There are fat little glass pots of homemade strawberry and apricot jam, blackberry jelly, and steaming jugs of hot coffee and milk. The younger members of my family stir some chocolate into their bowls. We drink from charming deep round breakfast bowls. Dunking chunks of crisp newly baked breadsticks into the bowl is part of the breakfast ritual. 'Le Toast' is also popular and uses up the previous day's bread. It is still considered quite sinful to throw away food in France, especially bread, and certainly it is a sign of bad housekeeping.

Lunch is a sit-down affair. We all wait for the head of the family to come home, then zoom in on the table to our allocated seats with our napkins in their individual pochettes (fabric pouch), each with different embroidered cross-stitched designs. My aunt and uncle sit in the centre of each side of the table. The seating is in order of seniority. The guests and the oldest members of the family are placed next to my aunt and uncle, and so on down the line.

The first course: some pates or terrines or some local sausage, or cold stuffed eggs or tomatoes filled with mayonnaise. Very simple, very fresh and very flavoursome. Plates are wiped clean with bread or if necessary changed, while we retain cutlery on a knife rest. Next is the meat, possibly with one hot vegetable. Another hot vegetable follows all this on its own; then a salad, such as cooked green beans with lashings of chopped parsley and French dressing made with lots of Grey Poupon mustard, or fresh soft lettuce. A large selection of cheeses follows — local cheeses as well as others from different provinces. There are always little treats and special efforts for us. Then follows the fresh fruit. And throughout the entire meal we have fresh bread, bought again just before the meal.

Local wine from the wine merchant is served in tall pewter pitchers. The younger members of the family have water or wine mixed with water. (Once you are sixteen or older you are allowed undiluted wine if you want it.) Although no one, as I recall, ever drinks excessive amounts of it, just a small glass or two which has little effect.

The fruit, cheeses, vegetables and wine are all stored in the cellars below the house. Being asked to fetch something for my aunt terrifies me. (Nowadays as I go down those steps, I recall the monsters and creatures that I imagined to be skulking around the corner.)

Afternoon tea consists of bread and chocolate — fresh bread again. We make four trips daily to the local bakery.

Regular suppliers of vegetables and fruit knock at our door to see if my aunt wants a case of peaches, basket of strawberries or a tray of grapes.

Dinner is at eight o'clock at night. We gather in the sitting room at about seven-thirty to catch up with each other's news of the day. A pre-dinner drink is offered: an aperitif — a glass of Dubonnet, St Raphael or similar herbal wine-based mixture. Dinner consists of a hot soup followed by a hot savoury dish to suit all ages such as a savoury flan, macaroni cheese or spinach souffle, but rarely meat, not for a family occasion. (Meat is so expensive that alternatives are devised.) Next, the inevitable salad, again with some light flavour-some dressing, to be followed by cheese, then dessert, with a platter of fruit for those who would like some.

In France, food is an important part of one's life. One must eat so why not do it in an enjoyable way? Lay the table nicely, sample one thing at a time, serve small portions. A large T-bone steak would be considered barbaric and over-indulgent.

My first visit to France with my husband, an Englishman, was a cause for celebration. (And ever since, any visit has, at some stage of the stay, included a large family reunion with up to twenty-six people sitting down at a long table for luncheon.) We ate local specialities, local foods, sampled un petit vin and talked and talked, using sign language with Guy which I translated.

During that first visit we drove across country, having the freedom to stop anywhere we fancied and sample the local cuisine, visit the irresistible markets, press our noses against the charcutier's window and be hypno-tised by the wealth of colour and texture in the mouth-watering cooked ready-to-take-away foods.

The provincial cuisines are varied and totally different in character. For example, the heady gustiness of Provence is quite different from the Germanic Alsace.

My mother's family is from La Rochelle while my father's family is from Tours, which is the capital city of Touraine, the Royal Province of the Princes, with its elegant chateaux dotted all along the Loire and the smaller rivers. Tours is the home of famous restaurateur Jean Barre. Touraine is referred to as the garden of France; rich in farmland, vineyards and orchards. Rivers and streams are alive with fish — pike and salmon in particular. The French spoken here is 'The French' (the equivalent I suppose of 'the Queen's English'). The goat cheese of St Maure is delicious and is eaten with the local red wine such as a Chinon, or a Bourgeuil.

Vegetables from this fertile farming area are sent to Paris. The aspara-gus in particular is highly prized and always the first of the season, being ready before asparagus grown on the lie de France.

In France, peaches are given all sorts of guises: ice creams, sorbets, peach sauce for puddings. The pulp is pureed or strained and mixed with castor sugar to taste and a dash of your favourite liqueur. Peaches appear in ice creams, sherbets, tarts, pies and flans. Prunes, on the other hand, appear in dessert or savoury dishes — rabbit, pork, fish, game and chicken. The prunes are seen in all the choclatiers' and patissiers' displays —: very large shiny fruit stuffed with prune puree mixed with cognac or liqueur. They melt in the mouth.

Visiting markets right across France, we watched women sniff and prod the vegetables and fruit, and saw how a good housewife would carefully weigh a rockmelon (cantaloup) in one hand and sniff it to test for sweetness and ripeness. Buying a really fresh local cheese, some fruit, some sausage, going to the cremerie to buy some butter, these are all simple pleasures that are a part of a holiday in the French countryside.

The butter in Brittany is deliciously creamy and salty, perfect with fresh crusty bread and local wine. The combination of ancient architecture, marvellous old farms, and carts and the variety of scenery, is a visual joy. And, with the local atmosphere and the food, the sum total is a richly satisfying experience. Much later I discovered the essence of Italy through the food and scenery of that country. But I have never recaptured the feeling of complete wellbeing that I had in France.

Some memories never fade. The fishy feasts we had in small restaurants and cafes in Quimper, in small coastal villages near the Pyrenees, in Brittany and Normandy. That special taste and texture of just caught, just cooked crabs, langoustes, shrimps, accompanied by light mayonnaise. Oysters galore: the large fat Belons and Marennes, and the small craggy shelled Portugaises — served on a bed of seaweed and crushed ice, as are mussels, whelks, limpets, clams and periwinkles. A speciality of Brittany called Andouille Bretonne is a favourite of mine — potent, rich smelly sausages made from strips of intestines and stomach stuffed into a sausage skin, poached or steamed and then grilled or fried.

One particular incident typifies, for me, the French approach to food. A few years ago I was in Langeais with some good friends, photographer Lewis Morley and Pat Morley and my daughter Stephanie. After much travelling we collapsed exhausted at a small hotel but we could not resist sampling the fare being offered. We ate well. Lewis chose a refreshing raspberry sorbet. Along came the waiter holding aloft an incredibly tall, slim conical mountain. Lewis couldn't manage to eat all of his portion.

Each of us in turn sampled this food from heaven. The waiter was most disappointed to see how little of it had been eaten. He turned to offer me some more and said when I declined, 'Madame, une toutepetite larme?' (a tiny teardropful). It was so charming. Here was a man who so loved the food he had to offer he couldn't bear to see it wasted.

With my mother in the family home, Barnes 1956

My Kitchen

The most important room in my house is without doubt the kitchen. I cannot imagine myself functioning in a kitchen too small to accommo-date a table or too small to have friends and family sitting around and chatting while I am cooking. I enjoy company and I'm not embarrassed by people looking on while I prepare a meal and it does not hamper my concentration.

I have had two kitchens which I feel I can call my own. The first was in London, the second in Australia. When we married, we moved into a flat in Shepherd's Bush with a borrowed round table, four chairs, a set of saucepans, a few bits of china and cutlery, a mattress and two armchairs from my mother-in-law. It was a spartan start to married life but a very enjoyable one. We both liked browsing in junk shops and ferreting for bargains. Slowly we gathered together some things chosen for their aesthetic appeal: old teapots, early nineteenth century earthenware plates, Victorian pub glasses. . . . Quite soon the kitchen was the most complete room. Complete because not only was it furnished but it was the room where one naturally gravitated. It was the focal point of our home.

During those years we managed to cram six, eight and even nine people around a small circular table; its diameter was no larger than a metre. I would cook around the guests, carefully lifting saucepans and frying-pans over their heads on my way to the sink. It was fun and in no way hampered one's enjoyment of the occasion.

Then we moved across the world to Australia, first to a flat and then to our first house. With the pleasure of having our own home came the painful process of renovating on a limited budget.

After two years came the big moment — the start of the kitchen. Friends helped us to knock the plaster off the walls. This was a surprisingly speedy operation, and also very rewarding for it revealed blocks of old thick sandstone in warm, golden hues.

With some inspired help from a talented Ukrainian carpenter we removed the plaster ceiling and lined the roof with pine. The sloping ceilings enlarged the room and gave it a farmhouse look.

I particularly wanted to capture a feeling of France. I had vivid memories of an aunt's ancient house, with the ceilings of its long, rambling rooms following the slope of the roof and floors tiled with old hexagonal terracotta tiles of incredible beauty. Finally, we man¬aged to find a floor finish that compared favourably with my aunt's hexagonal tiles — circular drain pipe caps, turned face down and set in a bed of cement. With the sandstone walls, timber cupboards and ceiling, they evoke the essence of a country kitchen.

The beams are hung with all kinds of frying-pans, saucepans, cocottes, cast-iron casseroles and many Chinese cane sieves used for steaming and straining food. Baskets on the floor are filled with onions, potatoes, oranges and pumpkins.

There are two ovens and grills side by side so I can easily bake a huge trout in one while sixteen individual souffles are in the other.

A small pantry cum appliance cupboard has rows of shelves for a large variety of teas. After dinner, herbal teas such as camomile, mint or vervenne make a pleasant change from coffee.

A brass clock on the wall tells the time as well as looking friendly. Two magnetised rods give me instant access to my extensive and ever-increasing collection of razor-sharp knives. Various bits and pieces such as wooden spoons in pots add to the general air of organised confusion.

Over the gas hot-plate, a huge copper hood soars up to the ceiling and whisks away all the fumes. The lighting is a combination of strips under shelves (hidden by wooden pelmets) and strategically placed spotlights.

The atmosphere of the kitchen is not isolated but part of the house as a whole. There are many things wrong with it — it is terribly congested yet there is plenty of space. Heads are likely to collide with the copper hood or a dangling frying-pan. There is not enough clear bench space. Nevertheless the kitchen is workable and has a warm personality. It has provided thousands of meals and survived years of test-cooking, and has gracefully matured and settled in as if it has been there for decades.

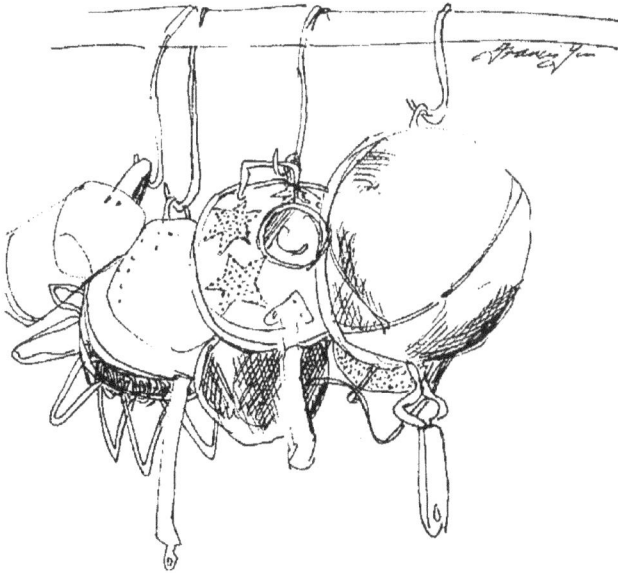

My first real kitchen, London 1959

On shopping

Our decision to come to Australia had my brother completely bemused. Being French, his immediate response was, 'Babette, you must be crazy. Just think of it, living without wine.' I persuaded myself that I was drinking my last glass of wine, eating my last leaf artichoke, that I would never again savour zucchinis or enjoy an eggplant or send myself into sheer ecstacy with a bowl of raspberries or some wild strawberries.

Once in Australia it took only a few hours to dispel these fears. Friends lent us their flat in Potts Point for our first weekend. We were reassured after peering into shops at nearby Kings Cross. They were crammed with eggplant, zucchinis, avocados, and fruit galore. The Viennese patisserie was packed with delectable goodies, and delicatessens overflowed with Italian and German bread, salamis and cheeses from all over the world. Very soon we discovered that not only was Australia heavily planted with the blessed vine, but also it produced superb wines — all this within three hours of walking off the S.S. Canberra.

We soon found that the ethnic food shops around the city and suburbs have much to offer. A visit to Leichhardt brings waves of nostalgia for Italy. I can buy freshly made pasta, calamari from the fish shop, fresh Italian cheeses — produce that reflects the food-buying habits of the locals.

For fresh fruit and vegetables I divide my loyalties between my local greengrocer at Hunter's Hill and that marvellous pair, Tom and Frank, who run a thriving business in, Oxford Street. Their trading policy is to stock whatever is in season anywhere in Australia. They supply many of the leading restaurants in Sydney and as a result stock many more unusual lines such as young tender sorrel, varieties of artichokes, fresh herbs, all types of capsicum, tomatoes, fresh figs, fresh dates, raspberries, black and red currants.

For fresh salmon eggs, smoked salmon, smoked eel and all kinds of unusual goodies, Cyril's Delicatessen is too temptingly close to my office. It is hard to resist when Cyril suggests trying something that is just in, such as smoked turkey legs. His sour cream and country butter are the best, as are his goose livers and boiling fowls.

The Chinese food shops are unlike any others and sell at-their-best fresh ginger, fresh water chestnuts for fruit stuffings for pork or stuffed eggplant, or sliced paper-thin into a salad. The snowpeas I use hot (barely cooked or steamed), or raw in a salad. They are delicious with the thinnest mushroom slices, fresh pears and fennel, all tossed in a light dressing of walnut or olive oil and lemon juice or flavoured vinegar. Their fresh coriander, which looks like a smaller leaf version of Italian parsley, is also excellent when chopped and used gener¬ously in salads. Their chives have an especially pungent flavour and in Chinatown you can also buy the very best watercress.

Superlative pork, fresh chicken livers and top quality chickens are other Chinatown specialities. Chickens are complete with heads and feet. I use the chickens to make chicken and vegetable soup and then reserve the boiled meat from the soup for a pie, pancake filling or to be eaten cold with a light lemony mayonnaise sauce.

For the freshest fish I go to my local fish markets in Rozelle or to Nicholas in Pyrmont and buy the best of the catch — baby sardines, whitebait, mussels, bream, a whole tuna or trevally, pearl perch, live crabs, sweet fat prawns.

I will drive across the city to buy a whole Italian cheese from the makers in Marrickville, to Deans in Double Bay for French cheese or choose from the wide selection at the Cheese Shop in Bondi Junction.

The best French cake shop in Australia is the Paris Cakeshop in Bondi, as their cakes have that authentic French flavour.

The freshest dried herbs, spices and Grey Poupon mustard in large quantities are found at the Bay Tree in Woollahra. They also have an extensive range of tempting cookery equipment and it is hard to pull oneself away, without buying something.

I miss the old Paddy's markets, where I used to buy cases of vegetables at closing time. I would bring home sixty capsicums to grill, peel and preserve in oil, or make enormous quantities of celery or beetroot soup to be eaten fresh, or frozen for later use.

Over the years I have collected wines from Len Evans Cellars, my local pub and with the help and advice of friends. A good selection is kept all over the house even under the bed and in my wardrobe.

The Way I Say I Care

As with everything else, one develops a style in cooking that is very personal. The character and person you are is evident in the way you present your food, prepare the meal, plan the menu. Some people do these things with gusto and generosity, others are studied and restrained, while some follow a discipline that could be considered nothing short of mean and stifling. If one is stingy with the quality and quantity, the meal will reflect that. The trick is to achieve the right balance, not to overdo it, yet not to be too restricted. In the planning of the meal, the food is selected to suit the occasion, making use of what is in season.

During cold weather I entertain in the dining-room, a small room with thick rough sandstone walls, a calico-tented ceiling below the tin roof and rough timber beams. The circular table can be extended by using a large top especially made for occasions when the numbers are ten or more. (It is magic, easy to handle, and when not in use, is simply rolled out of sight and put away.)

In warmer weather, the wide verandah is an ideal spot for up to sixteen people to talk, relax and enjoy each other's company and the meal at the long turn-of-the-century oak table.

The invitation could be for a weekend breakfast, lunch or dinner, more rarely to dinner during the week.

A gathering for breakfast at ten o'clock works well. Guests usually go home at one or two and have the rest of the day to do other things. Children can come with their parents which is also rather nice.

Fresh orange and champagne or apricot juice is the welcoming drink. The table is laid with a cloth and flowers; there are bowls of fresh fruit, a compote of guavas, or fresh sliced peaches coated with a puree of raspberries or strawberries. If the berries are not available fresh, bulk frozen ones can be used instead. One-and-a-half kilograms will make a delicious puree for sixteen. A platter of rockmelon with limes and bowls of Greek country-style yoghurt either plain or stirred into a puree of raspberries or strawberries is also good. The plain yoghurt is delicious with the fruit compotes, as is sour cream, or I will serve an Indian yoghurt drink, Lassi. This is followed by paper- thin pancakes with either grated Emmenthal, smoked salmon and sour cream and chopped dill or salmon eggs with sour cream and chopped chives — depending on what was served beforehand. Or I will make a spinach and cheese souffle.

LASSI (YOGHURT DRINK)

Use a liquidiser or food processor to make this drink on a hot summer's day. The yoghurt is thinned down with milk, water or fresh fruit juice such as orange, pineapple, carrot, grape or other refreshing juices. If the yoghurt is thinned down with water, add chunks of fresh peeled peaches, rockmelon, apricots, nectarines or strawberries and a little lemon juice or orange juice if necessary. (Sometimes we have plain yoghurt, water and lots of mint leaves with sugar to taste.)

If you don't have any electrical gadgets, use an egg beater to make a smooth drink, making a separate puree of fruit. Mint combines well with pineapple or orange but does tend to kill more delicate flavours.

FRESH PEACHES
WITH PUREED FRUIT

6 large or 8 medium juicy sweet peaches
5-6 cups berry fruits — fresh or frozen strawberries, raspberries or loganberries

Make a puree of the berry fruits in a food processor or a liquidiser, or put through a vegetable mill; sweeten to taste. Peel the peaches. If skinning them is difficult, plunge them into boiling water for 1 minute, peel and slice them and then immediately cover them with the pureed fruit to prevent browning. Chill and serve in a pretty, large bowl, or spoon into individual containers.

Serves eight.

French toast or Pop Overs can be served next, piping hot with maple syrup and crisp bacon, or honey and butter. I also serve French toast with butter and sugar or some freshly-made peach or strawberry jam and, of course, there will be lashings of freshly brewed coffee. Served with roast beef, Pop Overs are very good for mopping up meat juices and gravy.

POP OVERS

A very hot oven and well-greased muffin or pop over pans which must also be sizzling hot are absolutely necessary for making Pop Overs successfully. Preheat oven at 230°C (450°F).

Grease each pan with a rounded teaspoon of butter or bacon dripping for each Pop Over. Place in oven.

Mixture for one pan
  2 eggs
  Large pinch salt
  1 cup milk
  1 cup flour
  1 tablespoon oil or melted butteror bacon dripping

Beat the eggs until light and add the remaining ingredients. Beat until well blended, but don't overbeat. The batter should be the thickness of cream. Take the pans out of the oven. They must be sizzling hot. Fill each by one-third and quickly return to the hottest part of the oven, placing oven shelf as high as possible.

Bake for 20 minutes and then turn heat down to 190°C (375°F), and cook a further 15 to 20 minutes. Try one to see if they are ready. They must be crisp on the outside and moist inside.

For lunch or dinner the meals are more elaborate. A cold soup or some chilled cooked vegetables such as finger-size zucchinis, julienne of green beans, one or two slices of tomatoes, all carefully arranged on small plates, topped with a mustardy vinaigrette, sprinkled with grated Parmesan and chopped parsley. Or a platter of piping hot, just-made vegetable fritters covered with lashings of Emmenthal or generously sprinkled with parsley, or a spinach souffle. I thoroughly enjoy deciding what I will put with this or that. An unexpected find of crisp goose skin at a delicatessen will be heated and served on a mignonette salad as a first course, with a baked fish to follow. I enjoy cooking large fish — trout, trevally, or snapper, lightly stuffed with minced onion, ground almonds, a touch of finely chopped lemon peel, a little nutmeg, lots of butter rubbed inside and outside the fish. The fish is baked with a little white wine, served with beurre blanc, or with a light wine, egg yolk and lemon sauce. A whole stuffed tuna is delicious cooked in port and lemon juice.

Some delectable fillets of baby lamb from your favourite butcher can be simply roasted or pan fried with a little butter, a touch of garlic and rosemary. You could serve crown roast of lamb or a boned leg of lamb stuffed with an apricot mixture, cooked with fresh peaches or more dried apricots with wine, garlic and lemon; a roast of prime sirloin with bearnaise sauce or reduced sauce.

Skewered pork fillet rolls stuffed with liver, garlic, parsley and lemon peel is another favourite of mine, served with a platter of vegetables such as a puree of zucchinis.

STUFFED PORK FILLET ROLLS

This is such an easy and flavoursome dish, excellent served at any time of the year but especially so for large summer lunch gatherings, as it can be prepared in advance and needs very little supervision during cooking time. One roll will make a good serving for an average eater, two for a hearty eater.

Meat

12 small or 10 large pork fillets — serves 12

Stuffing

500 g of pigs liver*, minced or finely chopped

250 g of chicken livers, minced or finely chopped

2 cups soft white fresh breadcrumbs

2 eggs, beaten

1 tablespoon coarsely grated or finely chopped lemon peel

½ cup finely chopped parsley

1/3 cup finely chopped basil, or fresh mint or tarragon can replace the basil

3 large cloves garlic, crushed or very finely chopped

1 teaspoon freshly ground coriander

Salt and coarsely ground black pepper

*if you cannot buy pigs livers, use 750 g chicken livers

Mix all the stuffing ingredients together well.

Slice each pork fillet lengthways in three and beat with a mallet as you would escalopes of veal. Spread each slice on one side with the stuffing and roll up. Using 2 wooden skewers (metal will do if you don't have satay sticks), securely pierce through the centres of 2 rolls to prevent them from unrolling and to hold mixture in. Pile the rolls into a baking tin and cover until ready to cook.

Use a very large flat cast-iron griddle or a cooking sheet or a very wide frying-pan. Heat up a little olive oil and sear the rolls of pork on both sides for 2 to 3 minutes. Continue cooking for another 8 to 10 minutes on medium heat, or place in a hot oven at 200°C (400°F) in the hottest part of oven.

Seal the skewered meat rolls just before the arrival of your guests. Take the rolls out of the pan and keep them covered. Then 15 minutes before serving, put them into a hot preheated oven at 200°C (400°F) on large lightly oiled baking sheets.

Push on half-moon slice of lemon onto the end of each roll. Serve im-mediately on a thick bed of fresh watercress, parsley, basil or lettuce leaves and of course on hot plates. I usually accompany this with a puree of zucchinis.

PUREE OF ZUCCHINIS

12 large or 24 small zucchinis — serves 12
250 g butter
Salt
1 clove crushed garlic
White pepper

Put the zucchinis through the coarse grater of the food processor, or use the largest hole of a hand-grater. In a large wide-bottomed saucepan or a frying-pan, melt the butter and when hot but not turning colour, add the zucchinis, salt, garlic and white pepper. Stir constantly on a very hot heat, cooking for 3 minutes.

Sometimes I stir in 2/3 cup of finely chopped parsley or I replace the butter with 1 cup of sour or thick fresh cream. This method is even easier as the cream, garlic, zucchinis, salt and pepper are put in the pan before the guests arrive and left covered until ready to use. This takes about 5 minutes to heat through. Serve at once piping hot.

POTATO CASSEROLE

This dish always brings back memories of my childhood. It is so easy —just lots of slicing —then it is popped into the oven and you can forget about it until it is time to eat.

1 kg baby potatoes, washed and thinly sliced the thickness of a 20c piece (or a little thicker)

500 g smallish onions, peeled and thinly sliced

1 cup or more of milk

1 ½ cups cream

120 g butter

Salt and freshly ground pepper

In a deep casserole or souffle dish, place alternative layers of the potatoes and onion, dotting with small pieces of the butter and seasoning as you go along. Finish it off with a layer of potatoes. Pour over the cream and milk to just cover. Place in a low medium oven at 160°C (325°F), with the shelf placed half-way, and cook for 1 ¾ hours. This dish can be successfully reheated.

Serves 6.

Freshly milled pepper plays an important role, as does salt. I always make a point of having small pots of Maldon sea salt on the table, as I tend to under salt and I am not offended if people adjust the season¬ing to suit their palates. Cheeses are served on a large board covered with vine leaves or scented geranium leaves. The selection depends on what is available. A fresh piece of Brie, Camembert, a full flavoured Cheddar cheese, or any of the English cheeses such as the sage-flavoured Cheddar, Wensleydale, Caerphilly or some white or blue Castello, or simply a piece of my home-made quince cheese, juicy dried figs, dried or fresh dates, fresh lychees and grapes if in season.

My choice for dessert, sometimes prepared in advance, may be fresh fruit sorbet if the meal has been somewhat heavy, or souffle, pancakes, Summer Pudding, or a simple upside-down apple tart served warm with light vanilla custard. When raspberries are in season, I'll make a light bavarois topped with an egg custard sauce spiked with finely chopped crystallised ginger. This is a reversal of the usual order of ginger bavarois with raspberry sauce.

SUMMER PUDDING

Summer Pudding, laden with luscious berry fruits, is an extravaganza that never fails to be appreciated. For twenty-four people, I prepare two large puddings. The recipe given will serve twenty-four to thirty. For smaller numbers I cut back the recipe by half or by three-quarters.

I like to use stale sponge or make a French sponge like a Genoise cake to line the pudding basin. The traditional English version makes use of stale white bread with the crusts removed.

You will need two very large pudding basins or old-fashioned mixing bowls, enough slices (one centimetre thick) of sponge to completely line the basin and cover the top, seven kilograms of fruit for thirty people using raspberries, strawberries, red or black currants, youngberries.

4 to 5 kg raspberries (no stalks)

1 kg strawberries

1 kg youngberries or red currants

Castor sugar to taste

De-stalk and hull the fruit. Slice the strawberries in half. Put the fruit into separate bowls and sprinkle with the sugar. Leave for 1 hour. Have ready a basin or basins lined with sponge or stale bread. There must be no gaps. Slices must be evenly and attractively placed if using bread, as you will get the shape of the slice showing through. Overlap a little where necessary.

Ladle one layer of one kind of fruit, then the other and so on until you have reached the top, shaping into a shallow rounded mound, and cover closely with the remaining sponge or bread slices. Pour over as much of the juices as possible; cover with a layer of thin plastic or foil, and then put a flat plate or bottom of a cake tin on top, to just fit the diameter of the bowl. Place a weight on top. Refrigerate the pudding for 24 hours to allow the sponge to steep in the juices.

Carefully tip upside down onto a pretty, wide serving dish. I surround the pudding with a few fresh berries and place a few more on top. Sprinkled with white camomile flowers and blue borage flowers, it looks absolutely stunning. Serve it with a fresh vanilla egg custard thinned down with cream, or sour cream mixed with equal quantities of whipped cream, or simply running or whipped cream.

I prefer serving food on a platter so that guests can determine their own helpings. However, when serving large numbers of people, it is easier to present the first course on individual plates.

The wines are in the care of two or three male friends, and I concentrate on the food and the guests. Music is sporadic, depending on whether I take care of it or can persuade someone to be in charge!

Visual appeal is very important in a table setting, as long as it is supportive of the food and does not intrude. Table decoration is like a background 'prop' and contributes to the extravaganza of entertaining and extends an invitation to the guests to respond.

Lighting is also important. Candles cast a complimentary glow on the diners' faces. Candles can be supported on wall brackets, as well as being placed on the table. Centre lights and bright lights eliminate the possibility of creating a mood, as does one lonely candle bravely fighting to perform for the occasion.

I use the table as an extension of myself. With the food I give creatively and with love. With the way I set the table, I say I care.

(Top) Family picnic in the English countryside 1959;
(Lower) With Jocelyne van Heyst and friends celebrating
New Year in Hunters Hill 1971

Christmas

———————————•

Our Christmas is a ritual — a blend of English and French traditions. I experienced my first French Christmas in France in 1976 when I took the children, Arabella, Sholto and Stephanie, to spend a month en famille. With first and second cousins and nephews and nieces the family totalled more than sixty.

At the house in Nevers every room, right up to the attic bedrooms, was filled with members of the Bayle clan. The French have their feast at 1 a.m. after Midnight Mass on Christmas Eve. We waited for those who had gone to church to return, and then sat down to a selection of cold dishes, oysters, pates, cold rare roast beef, duck, preserved goose, cheeses, fresh fruits and moist dates and prunes just stuffed with freshly made marzipan.

After dinner the room was cleared, the furniture pushed aside and everyone who was to be there the next day had to leave a pair of shoes or boots. There were twenty-one pairs arranged in a semi-circle in several rows around the tree. Around them were placed the presents intended for the respective owners.

In the morning, after a hasty breakfast we impatiently waited for my uncle to make his appearance at eleven as no one was allowed in the dining-room until he arrived. Then we all formed a queue in order of head height, the littlest at the front, while my uncle went in — the room was in total darkness — to light the dozens of sparklers attached to the Christmas tree. This was the cue for Arabella to lead us in, all gasping at the silvery splendour of the tree and the mountains of presents on the floor.

Christmas luncheon, served mid-afternoon, consisted of pate defoie, platters of oysters, stuffed geese with chestnut and apple sauce, vegetables, a salad, cheeses, Buche de Noel, Mousse au Chocolate, and fruit and nuts. That, I thought, is that, little thinking anyone could contemplate dinner. A supper followed at 10 p.m.!

In Australia, our Christmas is very different. The hot weather gives one an opportunity to vary the menu and to include a number of cold dishes. Our breakfasts of croissants, brioches, apricot jam, fresh fruit and coffee have been a Hayes' tradition for twenty years or more.

Luncheon is the main meal, always with a group of friends and an ever-stretching table. The table is set as elaborately as possible with masses of flowers, crackers (bon-bons) and a miniature nativity scene. Music in the background is in stiff competition with the cicadas, and the heat of the sun is tempered by the water-sprinklers in the garden.

*Smoking a cigarette!!! I dig into some sweet
goodies at the end of another family picnic 1957*

EGGNOG

To start the festivities, depending on the weather, I will serve a champagne or an eggnog. The eggnog is made with 24 egg yolks, beaten until thick, with 2 tablespoons of sugar per egg, to which 1 add 2 litres of cream and 2 of milk and 1 of brandy or whisky, then the beaten egg whites are folded in and the whole is a topped with freshly grated nutmeg. It's very rich and very festive, and a reminder of Christmas in Europe.

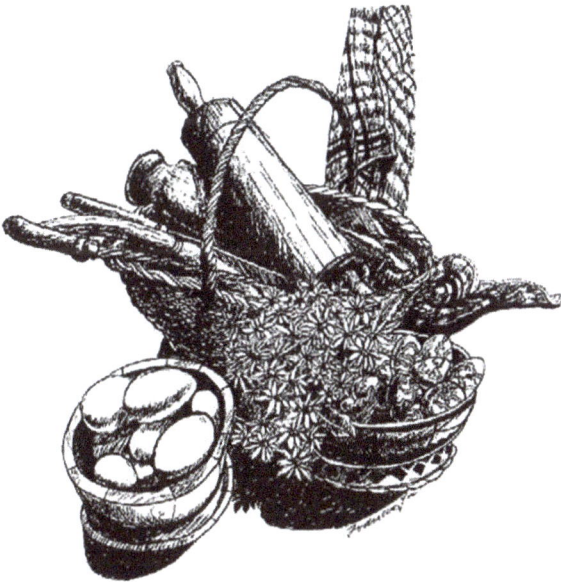

If it is very hot we will have iced soup, watercress, cucumber or cream of carrot for the first course. Then an enormous platter of oysters, mussels, prawns, yabbies, Balmain bugs, pipis (cockles), and lobster tails on crushed ice, accompanied by bowls of light, lemony mayonnaise. An alternative for cool weather would be one of my mother's Christmas recipes, Shellfish in Cream Wine Sauce.

SHELLFISH IN CREAM
WINE SAUCE

Per person you will need:
3 large green prawns, peeled and deveined,
4 oysters, and 4 scallops (keep the coral aside)
For the sauce:
5 tablespoons butter
½ cup finely chopped onion
2 tablespoons flour
A litre or so of fish stock
1 1/3 litre good white burgundy or riesling
Salt and white pepper
1 cup cream (226 g or 8oz cup) beaten together with 4 egg yolks
Some finely chopped parsley

Peel the prawns, and place all the peelings in saucepan covered with ¾ litre water and boil gently to make a stock. Reduce the liquid to ½ litre. Add a bayleaf and some parsley stalks if you have these. Melt the butter, add the onion and cook gently until transparent; be careful they don't brown at all! Stir in the flour until smooth, take off heat and slowly pour in the hot strained fish stock. Return to heat and stir and when thickened slowly pour in the wine. Cook, gently simmering for 20 minutes. Strain through a fine sieve and return to the pan. Put in the prawns, and bring to the boil gently, turn down heat and simmer for 2 minutes. Add the scallops and oysters and simmer for 2 more minutes. Pour in the cream and egg mixture and gently stir over low heat to prevent curdling and so as not to break up the shellfish. Don't stop stirring until the sauce has thickened. Serve in a shallow heated quiche dish or pie dish and sprinkle with the parsley. Serves 8.

The seafood will be followed by a simple roast of rare fillet of beef, guinea fowl, chicken (which the children favour cooked with lemon juice and tar-ragon), lamb, veal — and a salad of sliced juicy pears, watercress, fennel, snowpeas, chopped chives, parsley with a lemon and olive-oil dressing.

For Christmas meat dishes I aim to produce something a little different to follow the shellfish. There is always a selection.

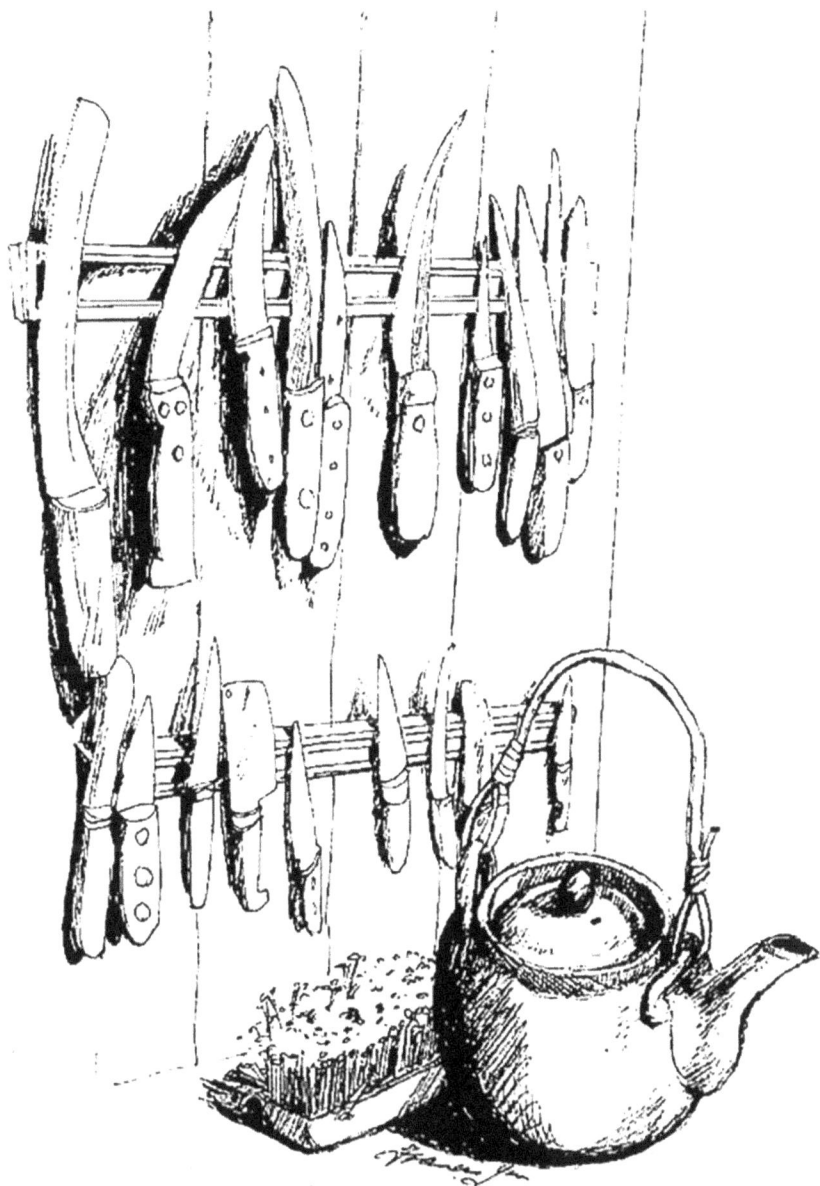

Typical food for friends at Hunters Hill in the 1970s

LAMB WITH PLUMS

A case of luscious plums left on my doorstep by generous friends inspired me to produce this concoction during a festive season.

This dish can be prepared in advance and left covered at room temperature or in a larder. Try not to refrigerate it. Serve just one vegetable with this - snake beans or tender runner beans are delicious.

For 12 people

2 kg of firm new-season plums (Victoria, Damson or any acid plums)
½ cup water Sugar to taste
4 loins of lamb boned with flat tail ends and fat cut off left whole
60 g butter
24 small onions, peeled
Salt
2 tablespoons good wine vinegar
1 teaspoon freshly ground coriander
Some scented geranium leaves or watercress or fresh basil to decorate serving dish.

Wash and stone the plums. Cook with the water and just enough sugar to sweeten the fruit, until the plums are soft - about 15 minutes. Cool, then crush the fruit lightly with the back of a wooden spoon. Melt the butter in a heavy frying-pan, and lightly brown the onions all over on medium heat for 4 to 5 minutes, and remove from the pan while browning the meat. Brown the meat, two loins at a time on fairly strong heat. Place the meat side by side in 2 roasting pans, and pour half the stewed plums and the onions over each pan. Sprinkle the meat with the salt, vinegar and coriander and set aside until ready to cook.

Forty-five minutes before serving, place the meat in the hottest part of a pre-heated oven at 200°C (400°F) and after 15 minutes lower the heat to

160°C (325°F). If placing the meat in the oven straight after browning, cook 5 minutes less.

Take the meat out of the pan, and carve it into round neat slices 1½ cm thick. Lay in a neat row down the centre of an oval serving dish. (When serving twelve people, I like to put the meat on two heated platters to save waiting time.) Adjust the seasoning of the sauce and spoon the very hot plums and juices over the meat —you will have lots so use it all. Decorate with geranium leaves or whatever is available — sometimes I use sprigs of mint.

LOIN OF VEAL WITH CHEESE

This is an easy dish to prepare, particularly so for beginners who worry about timing.

1 or 2 chops per person depending on appetite

1 thin slice (1/2 cm) Emmenthaler cheese per chop, or Gruyere, cut same size as meat

1 heaped coffee spoon hot

French mustard, e.g. Dijon

A few caraway seeds

Have a loin of veal, to serve 4 or more, chined by the butcher for easy carving. Ask him to slice partially through the loin to allow you to sandwich slices of cheese in between each one. Butter a roasting tin lavishly. Place the meat on top, firmly wedge a slice of the cheese between each chop, and tuck well into the meat as it must cook inside the meat. Place the meat on the roasting pan with the fat facing up; smear lavishly with the mustard. If liked, sprinkle caraway seeds lightly over the top. Place in hot oven —preheated to 200°C (400°F) — on the middle shelf, lowering the temperature to 160°C (325°F) after 15 minutes.

Baste the meat with the pan juices and leave it for 40 minutes or so until done, depending a little on thickness of the loin.

Cut into slices where the bone has been sawn through, place on a hot platter covered with watercress, sorrel leaves, basil leaves, or on a bed of thin sauteed potatoes. Serve at once — don't delay.

Have a loin of veal, to serve 4 or more, chined by the butcher for easy carving. Ask him to slice partially through the loin to allow you to sandwich slices of cheese in between each one. Butter a roasting tin lavishly. Place the meat on top, firmly wedge a slice of the cheese between each chop, and tuck well into the meat as it must cook inside the meat. Place the meat on the roasting pan with the fat facing up; smear lavishly with the mustard. If liked, sprinkle caraway seeds lightly over the top. Place in hot oven —preheated to 200°C (400°F) — on the middle shelf, lowering the temperature to 160°C (325°F) after 15 minutes.

Baste the meat with the pan juices and leave it for 40 minutes or so until done, depending a little on thickness of the loin.

Cut into slices where the bone has been sawn through, place on a hot platter covered with watercress, sorrel leaves, basil leaves, or on a bed of thin sauteed potatoes. Serve at once — don't delay.

SAUTEED POTATOES

Boil small potatoes the day before or at least 8 hours before they are needed. Peel, cool and slice ½ cm thick. Melt butter in a wide frying-pan and tip potatoes in. Add salt and pepper, and turn potatoes over when they are browned. These are delicious cooked with 2 to 3 tablespoons of chopped onion, or if you have not flavoured the meat with caraway seeds, add a little of your favourite herb during cooking.

Next there will be two vast cheeseboards with quinces, lychees, dried muscat grapes, and bowls of iced cherries. Dessert is something sharp like a grapefruit or lemon fluff. Then come the mince pies with brandy butter, and Christmas pudding flamed and decorated with holly, followed by bowls of cherries, peaches, apricots, nectarines on ice. After the food, presents are exchanged.

GRAPEFRUIT FLUFF

4 large fresh eggs, separated
4 rounded tablespoons castor sugar
1 packet (10 g) gelatine
½ cup hot water
¾ cup grapefruit juice (or lemon orange fruit puree or 1 of plum puree)
Beat the yolks and the sugar together to a pale and thick consistency. Sprinkle the gelatine into the hot water and dissolve thoroughly. Add to the fruit juice. Then stir into the yolk mixture. Chill the mixture until it thickens enough to hold the stiffly beaten egg whites. Fold the stiffly beaten egg whites into the mixture and leave it to set for 4 hours. You can use a mould for this if you prefer. Serves 10.

Coffee is served with stuffed fruit — dates, peaches, apricots and figs are stuffed with marzipan made from almonds; or pistachios mixed with sugar and bound with egg whites, then rolled in sugar and put into small paper

Brunch on the verandah at Hunters Hill
with the table typically set to welcome friends, 1971

One of our roadside picnics with our 1927 Bentley while on the way to visit my family in Le Mans 1963

Picnics

I always associate picnics with large groups of people — parents and children, single friends and friends without children. We are all guests and hosts at an outdoor party. The responsibility for the success of the outing lies within every participant. It's a relaxed happy group activity of the very nicest kind.

My memories of picnics date from my childhood in England. They were small outings with parents and one or two friends. The meal was stretched through the day with walks in the woods and fields, picking wildflowers, lying in the sun or the shade, talking and reading. We had terrines, pates, roast meats, good wines, cheeses and fresh fruit laid out on a tablecloth — all the trappings that go with French-style picnics.

In France, picnics were opportunities for family get-togethers. A half-way point would be picked on the map and everyone would converge from Tours, Le Mans, Nevers, Montpelier, Chamonix and Dijon. From all points of the compass would come sisters, brothers, cousins, nephews and nieces armed with baskets of goodies, and the queen of them all, my tiny, frail grandmother. This way the evergrowing, on-the-move members of my father's family were able to catch up with each other and reaffirm their warm, loyal, caring bonds.

England, in those days, always seemed to be deficient in hot sunny days. A fire was always necessary. Picnics were never cancelled because of bad weather. They usually started at lunchtime and went on well after the sun had set. We would cook large pieces of marinated meat over the coals, bring soup in thermoses and mull some wine. Everyone contributed food, wine and a sense of fun. After lunch we would have a hearty game of rounders to exercise ourselves and recover for the evening meal. We would not leave for home until the rush-hour traffic was over and in the meantime enjoyed a hot snack with some freshly-made tea or coffee. The coffee was brewed over the hot coals.

In Australia I have learnt that picnics are best in autumn, winter and spring. One favourite spot is near a creek, with large pools deep enough to swim in. During the cooler months we have a fire. We gather fourteen to twenty-six people with children to enjoy a day of friendly exchanges, good food washed down with wine, water or fruit juices, depending on preferences and age.

I spend a little bit of time ringing up friends to ensure that everyone contributes to a different area of the meal for balance and variety. The nice thing is that people care enough to make something special.

On a typical occasion, Pat made a delicious rabbit terrine. Maggi prepared a potato pie. Margaret fought her way along a densely overgrown bush track, carrying a superb French fruit flan and a fruit tart richly layered with custard. Vicky brought an exquisitely arranged Victorian basket of freshest, in-their-prime fruits and her famous Russian carrot cake. Edwina had her delicious Indonesian chicken curry to be eaten with Lebanese breads, and my neighbour Dagmar brought all kinds of Czecho-slovakian delicacies. My contribution was satay sticks or kebabs, cooked over coals, and soups. A rare roast beef was sliced on the spot and followed by zucchini salad. Fresh crusty bread, cheeses and delicacies brought by everyone finished off the meal.

We never stay into the evening. Somehow, the hot sun, the exhilarating fresh air, and the problems of fighting one's way through an overgrown bush path in the dark seem to discourage the thought.

ALBERT STREET TERRINE

Pat is fortunate enough to live in a lively and colourful Italian district of Sydney and even more fortunate to have generous neighbours who work every square centimetre of their back garden. There are neat rows of vegetables, and vegetable-bearing vines cover the back verandah. She frequently finds herself the receiver of a tender rabbit or a well-run chicken. Pat marinated a rabbit overnight for a terrine and combined it with walnuts and vegetables to achieve a layered look which looks attractive when cut. Its rich variety of textures makes it good eating too! She likes to marinate the meat to give it a fuller flavour.

1 fat rabbit, jointed strips of flesh

Marinate this in —

½ bottle red wine

1 large onion sliced

3 cloves garlic, crushed

2 bay leaves

1 teaspoon ground allspice

1 teaspoon each of salt and pepper

Heat the marinade and simmer for a few minutes. Then pour it over the rabbit which has been placed in a flat basin, to blanch the meat. Place in the fridge overnight.

Drain the rabbit, reserving the marinade. Roll strips in 1 tablespoon of chopped parsley and set aside.

For the terrine

500 g pork neck, finely minced with sinews discarded

250 g smoked speck (streaky smoked bacon), cut into small cubes

750 g bacon rashers

½ cup soft breadcrumbs

2 small eggs

1 clove garlic, crushed

1 chopped onion

3 chopped sticks celery

150 g green stuffed pimento olives, halved

150 g walnut pieces

1 teaspoon fresh ground black pepper

½ teaspoon salt (used sparingly)

½ teaspoon sage

1 teaspoon thyme

1 teaspoon mace

4 teaspoons fresh herbs made up of 2 parsley, 1 coriander, 1 mint

1 teaspoon of dill (optional)

Grated rind of 1 lemon and ½ orange

Mix together all the dry ingredients (spices, breadcrumbs etc.). Add all the meat and mix together with the eggs and ½ cup of the marinade. Make sure the mixture is not too wet. Butter a terrine (or a 2 litre deep loaf tin or baking dish). Lay bacon rashers in the dish, overlapping the edges to cover the entire contents when finished. Divide pork mixture into three. Put in a layer of pork mixture, then layer half of the rabbit strips lengthways, then a layer of pork; press down well. Add a final layer of rabbit and then a final layer of pork on top. Press down well and wrap the bacon rashers over the top.

Dish should be approximately 2/3 full, with a mound in the middle. Cover with buttered paper, then cover with a lid of foil.

Place the dish in a tray of hot water and put into a preheated oven of 160°C (325°F). Cook for 2 to 2½ hours. When cooked there will be liquid. Take out of oven, cool, and pour off excess liquid. Cover tightly and refrigerate overnight before eating.

DADA'S ORANGE PICNIC DESSERT CAKE

A delightfully moist and flavoursome cake that can be made (by doubling or trebling) into a large cake, and is ideal for the afternoon tea session of a picnic, or as a dessert. It is also delicious served with sour cream mixed with equal quantities of whipped cream.

125 g soft butter

½ cup sugar

1 rounded dessertspoon of grated orange rind

2 eggs

3 tablespoons brandy or whisky

1 cup semolina

1 level teaspoon baking powder

125 g ground almonds

Preheat the oven to 200°C (400°F). Prepare a 20 cm cake tin, buttered and lined with buttered greaseproof paper.

Cream butter, sugar and orange rind until light and fluffy. Thoroughly beat in each egg, one at a time, then the brandy or whisky.

Sift the semolina, baking powder and ground almonds together and stir into the mixture, combining thoroughly, and tip into the prepared tin. Put into the centre of the oven, lower heat to 180°C (350°F) and bake for 30 minutes. In the meantime prepare the syrup.

1 ¼ cups orange juice

½ cup sugar

2 tablespoons Grand Marnier, Cointreau or brandy

Put juice and sugar into a saucepan. Bring to the boil and boil briskly to thicken for 5 minutes. Take off heat, add the liqueur.

Take cake out of oven, turn upside down onto a baking dish and pour the syrup over it. Return to the oven and cook another 15 minutes.

MULLED WINE

Ideally I prefer to serve this on winter picnics preparing it over an open fire. We usually have a fire to cook our satay sticks or kebabs and of course to make the billy tea! For those not planning to light a fire, prepare it at home and keep hot in a thermos.

I use red or white wine or both, depending on what flagon wine I have and the number of people. The secret is not to boil the mixture but to heat it to just below boiling point. Sweeten to taste and add (for a flagon or 3 bottles):

1 tablespoon whole cloves

4 small cinnamon sticks crumbled 1 coffee spoon grated nutmeg

1 lemon and 1 orange, peeled and cut into small cubes

Bring to just below boiling point and serve, or put into a thermos

I suppose I found my identity through my love of food. Right from childhood, I was always out of step with my geographical location — a French girl in Syria, a foreigner in London during my teen years, an English cousin when I went back to France for holidays and an English/French woman by the time I came to Australia.

My gipsy-like existence is at an end now; the camp site in Sydney is definitely permanent. I'm entirely relaxed and contented here. But throughout my life I have looked to my French background for reassurance.

Entertaining in the French manner gave me a sense of security and stability that I probably lacked. I have elected to view my passionate interest in food as fulfilling and creative as opposed to neurotic and compensatory. The satisfaction I derive from cooking for others is my kind of 'high', so I guess I'm a gregarious cook.

With the very freshest of what's available I let the ingredients inspire me. Then comes the thrill of putting it together, when I feel joyous, light-headed! And the shared experience of eating with friends and family further extends the pleasure.

With my children, (from left); Stephanie, Sholto and Arabella

OTHER BOOKS IN THE
SYDNEY-PARIS LINK SERIES:

Paul Wenz
A Coral Eden
Diary of a New Chum
Their Father's Land
The Thorn in the Flesh

Tom Thompson
Australasian Artists at the French Salons

Alister Kershaw
Village to Village
One for the Road

Leon Ducharme
Journal of a Political Exile in Australia
Xavier Prieur
Notes of a Convict of 1838

Robert Wallace
To Catch A Forger
An Axe to Grind
Paint Out
Finger Play

Jean-Claude Lesage
Australian Painters in Etaples

www.ingramcontent.com/pod-product-compliance
Lightning Source LLC
Chambersburg PA
CBHW051209090426
42740CB00021B/3440